Little
MONSTER
Mazes

Viki Woodworth

Dover Publications, Inc.
Mineola, New York

Bibliographical Note

Little Monster Mazes is a new work, first published by Dover
Publications, Inc., in 2006.

International Standard Book Number

ISBN-13: 978-0-486-45189-3
ISBN-10: 0-486-45189-5

Manufactured in the United States of America
Dover Publications, Inc., 31 East 2nd Street, Mineola, N.Y. 11501

Note

Everyone has somewhere to go—especially Little Monsters! In each of the forty-eight mazes in this little book, a Little Monster has some place to go, or something to find. You will help the Little Monsters by showing them the way through the maze. Just draw a line from Start to End in each puzzle. Use a pencil so that you can erase your line if you have gone the wrong way.

Try to complete all of the mazes before checking the Solutions, which begin on page 52. You can have even more fun by coloring in the finished puzzles with colored pencils or crayons. Good luck!

Little Monster wants to walk Smiley, her dog. Help her find the way to the end of the maze to get to Smiley.

Whiskers has run away, and Little Monster would like to help her get home. Show Little Monster the way.

This Little Monster looks lost! Help him find the right path to take to get to the end of the maze.

Help Little Monster find the way to get to the flowers so that she can water them.

That bowl of cereal looks yummy! Little Monster has his spoon—help him get to the cereal.

8

start

end

Help Little Monster find the path to take to finish the snowman. Hurry! It's cold!

9

It's time to fill up the tank in Little Monster's car.
Show her the way to the gas pump.

10

Little Monster knows that he can mail his letter at the end of the path. Help him get there.

11

There's a basket of eggs at the end of the maze. Take Little Monster along the path to the eggs.

Little Monster is thirsty, and there's some fresh, cool milk at the end of the path. Help him get to it.

13

Waaa! Baby Monster wants his bottle! Show Little Monster the way to get to her little brother.

14

Little Monsters brush their teeth after meals. Help
this Little Monster find the tube of toothpaste.

It's raining, and Little Monster needs her boots.
Please show her how to get to them.

Little Monster is collecting seashells. Help her get to the pile of shells so she can put them in her basket.

end

start

This Little Monster has a bone for Pokey. Show Little Monster the path to take to get to Pokey.

That ice cream sundae looks yummy! Help Little Monster find the way to get to it.

Lucky is wearing Little Monster's sunglasses! Show Little Monster how to get to Lucky.

20

Little Monster just remembered where he parked his bicycle. Show him how to get to it.

This Little Monster doesn't like waves! Help her paddle to the end of the maze, where the water is calm.

22

Those cookies smell delicious! Little Monster will be glad if you help him get to the cookies.

The sun is shining at the end of the path. Help Little Monster find her way to the sunshine.

Little Monster is tired of swimming. Take him to the steps at the end of the pool.

At the end of the path is a piggy bank. Show Little
Monster how to get there so she can save her money.

Help Little Monster get to the end of the path. He has parked his toy car there and wants to take a ride.

The baby bird has flown out of its cage. Show Little Monster how to get to the bird and bring it home.

Little Monster is ready for a sled ride. Help her ride all the way to the end of the path.

The silly puppy has taken Little Monster's shoe.
Please take Little Monster to her shoe.

It's Little Monster's birthday! Won't you show her the way to get to her cake?

Little Monster needs to cut out some pictures. Take him to the pair of scissors at the end of the path.

32

The pet fish has escaped! Help Little Monster get to the end of the path and rescue his pet.

These friends want to play in the park. Help one Little Monster find the right path to get to his friend.

34

This sleepy Little Monster wants to get into his cozy
bed. Show him how to find it at the end of the path.

35

There's a cool pool at the end of the slide. Help Little Monster go down the slide and take a dip in the pool.

36

Little Monsters love to bowl. Help this Little Monster roll the ball to the end and hit the pins.

This Little Monster cowgirl wants to ride her pony. Show her the way to get to it.

38

A bubble bath is just what this Little Monster needs!
Take him along the path to the bathtub.

You need a tennis ball to play tennis. Help Little Monster find the tennis ball so he can start the game.

Mushrooms are growing at the end of the path. Show Little Monster the way to get to them.

Little Monster is in a runaway balloon. Please help his mother get to him before he floats away!

Take Little Monster to the end of the path so that she can write in her notebook.

Skating is fun, but this Little Monster would like the hot cocoa at the end of the path. Help her get to it.

44

Help Little Monster get to the end of the path so that she can throw the basketball.

Quick! Help Little Monster get to her balloon before
it flies away.

Take Little Monster to the airport at the end of the maze. He's ready to land his plane!

This Little Monster loves to paint. Please help her find her paints at the end of the path.

Those strawberries smell sweet! Show Little Monster how to get to them.

49

Little Monster left her dance shoes at the end of the path. Take her to them so she can dance.

50

end

start

Do you see that lollipop at the end of the maze? Please show Little Monster how to get to it. Thank you!

Solutions

page 4

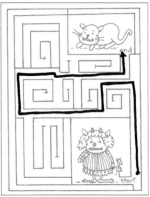

page 5

page 6

page 7

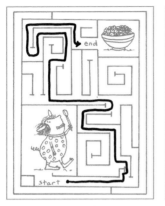

page 8

page 9

page 10

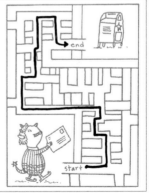

page 11

page 12

page 13

page 14

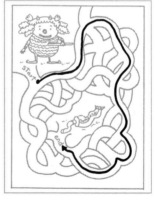

page 15

page 16

page 17

page 18

page 19

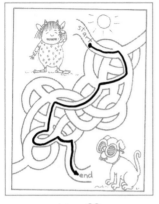

page 20

page 21

page 22

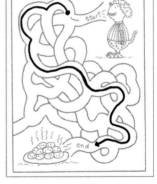

page 23

page 24

page 25

page 26

page 27

page 28

page 29

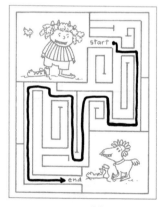

page 30

page 31

page 32

page 33

page 34

page 35

page 36

page 37

page 38

page 39

page 40

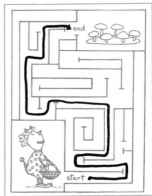

page 41

page 42

page 43

61

page 44

page 45

page 46

page 47

page 48

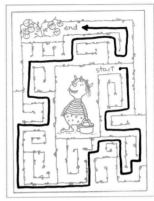

page 49

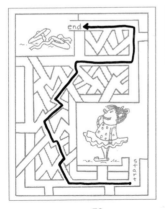

page 50

page 51